WHY DO CATS DO THAT?

Real Answers to the Curious Things Cats Do

by Kim Thornton

illustrations by Keith Robinson

BOWTIE™ PRESS

A Division of Fancy Publications

Library of Congress Catalog Card Number: 96-80217
ISBN: 1-889540-02-1

BowTie™ Press
3 Burroughs
Irvine, California 92618

Printed and bound in Singapore

First Printing January 1997

10 9 8 7 6

Contents

Why Do Cats Purr?

People love the sound of a cat's purr, but the soothing sound is still not very well understood. You probably think a purring cat is a happy cat, but this explanation doesn't cover all the bases. Cats purr not only when they are happy but also when they are stressed—for instance, at the veterinarian's office. Think of the purr as the cat's equivalent of our smile, indicating that no hostile intent is meant.

How cats purr has long been a mystery. In a Breton folktale, cats are said to have developed the purr after spinning 10,000 skeins of linen thread to help a princess break an enchantment. It's easy to understand how a cat's purr could be compared to the whir of a spinning wheel.

Today, however, the mystery has been solved. The sound a cat makes is caused by vibrating muscles surrounding the larynx. Researchers have also discovered where the purr originates: in the brain. Stimulation of a specific area in the cat's brain causes cats to begin purring.

The purr is one of the first sounds newborn kittens make, no doubt as they snuggle up to their mother for suckling and warmth. As they mature, their purr becomes more complex. While young cats tend to purr in monotone, adults are capable of reaching two or three

It was once believed that the big cats did not purr, but experts have discovered that wild members of the felis genus, which includes bobcats, cougars, and lynxes, can purr like domestic cats. Members of the genus panthera—lions, tigers, leopards, panthers, and jaguars—can purr, but only with outward breaths, unlike domestic cats, who can purr while inhaling and exhaling. The difference may be a matter of throat construction.

notes and sometimes as many as five. Purring can go on for hours without a break, even while a cat is eating or sleeping. In fact, it has been suggested that the purr is nothing more than a form of snore. Often, purring cats drool as well. The combination of salivation, purring, and paw kneading in an adult cat may indicate a temporary regression to feeding time in kittenhood.

What is the purpose of the purr? I don't think it has one. I think the purr is the sound of the motor that runs the cat.

Why Do Cats' Eyes Glow in the Dark?

A cat's unusually large eyes are perhaps his most striking features, and never more so than at night, when they seem to glow in the dark with an almost supernatural light. The cat is a nocturnal prowler, and his powerful sense of vision is what makes him so successful. But how exactly do the eyes work? Can a cat really see in the dark, using only those glowing eyes? Well, not quite. Here's how it works.

The feline eye structure includes the cornea, which is the clear, curved part of the eyeball in front of the pupil; the iris, which gives the eye its color; the lens, located behind the iris; the retina, consisting of a network of light-sensitive cells; and the tapetum lucidum, a Latin term that translates as "bright carpet." The cornea, lens, and retina work in much the same way as a camera. The cornea acts as the viewfinder, taking in light and transmitting it to the lens. The lens bends the light rays, focusing them to form an image on the retina.

Where does the tapetum lucidum come in? It is what allows the cat to take in extra light in dim situations. Lining most of the back of the retina, the tapetum lucidum acts as a mirror, reflecting light that was not absorbed the first time it passed through the retina. The result is the glow, called eye shine, that you see when light strikes your cat's eyes in

a darkened room. A cat can see no better than you or I when in a situation of total darkness, but when some light is present, the tapetum lucidum allows the cat to make better use of it.

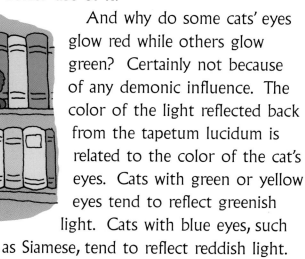

And why do some cats' eyes glow red while others glow green? Certainly not because of any demonic influence. The color of the light reflected back from the tapetum lucidum is related to the color of the cat's eyes. Cats with green or yellow eyes tend to reflect greenish light. Cats with blue eyes, such as Siamese, tend to reflect reddish light.

Why Do Cats Sleep so Much?

Sleep, eat, sleep, play, eat, sleep. Sleep a little more. Dream about mousearoni, mouseburgers, moussaka. Eat. Sleep some more. This feline schedule is no exaggeration. Cats sleep up to 18 hours a day, much more than most other mammals. Such a restful lifestyle is not limited to domestic cats. Wild cats have been described as living a life of inactivity punctuated by searches for food. It's clear that house cats see no reason to alter this way of life.

It's not known why cats sleep so much. Perhaps it is related to their solitary nature. Apart from lions, who live in groups called prides, cats are the Greta Garbos of the animal world: they want to be alone. And since they don't read or watch television, they do the next best thing: sleep. You might say that cats are the original couch potatoes.

How much sleep a cat gets depends on his stage of life and his lifestyle. Kittens and old cats sleep the most. A warm, well-fed, contented cat will sleep just about any time. Cats who are confined, such as those in catteries or boarding kennels, while away the hours with catnaps. Cats normally sleep in brief spurts, but cats whose owners work full-time may sleep all day, saving their waking hours for morning and evening, when they can socialize with their people.

Do our cats dream? Yes, they do, and they are as active in a dream state as they are when they're awake, twitching,

Despite the fact that cats are such experienced sleepers, they are as good as alarm clocks—and sometimes worse. If you don't want your cat waking you up every day at four in the morning to feed him, never respond to his pleas, not even once. Cats learn very quickly, and once they realize they can get you out of bed by yowling or meowing, you're history. Teach your cat to let sleeping people lie.

swishing their tails, and making noise. What are they dreaming about? Well, unless they start talking in their sleep we'll never know, but my guess is that they're finally catching that elusive and mocking sparrow out in the backyard. Or maybe they're just reliving their latest meal.

12

Why Do Cats Always Land on Their Feet?

Cats have a legendary ability to land on their feet after a fall. But is it true that cats always land on their feet? That depends, interestingly enough, on the height from which they fall.

When cats fall, they rely on two organs to bring them down safely: their eyes, which help cats position themselves correctly; and their vestibular apparatus, located in the inner ear, which controls balance and orientation. An automatic sequence of motions goes into play when a cat topples. First, the cat rights her head. Then she rotates the front half of her body 180 degrees. Once the front legs are facing down, the cat rotates the

rear half of her body and flattens out so as to help spread the area of impact. The tail acts as a counterbalance. As the cat hits the ground, she arches her back in an attempt to help cushion the impact.

Why does the height from which a cat falls make a difference? Falling from a great height allows more time for this sequence of motion to take place. Cats who fall from shorter distances are often hurt more severely because they don't have time to react properly. And why do cats fall from high places? Mainly, it's because their depth perception isn't very good. Apparently, they don't realize they're about to jump eight stories instead of eight feet.

Just because a cat survives a long-distance fall doesn't mean she can't be injured. Broken legs are a common result of falls, so kids, don't try this at home. Your cat will thank you.

Why Do Cats Scratch the Furniture?

Does your pet have cat scratch fever? No, not the disease; the desire to claw only the finest furniture, wallpaper, and draperies. Well, you're not alone. Scratching is an innate feline behavior, and it is something that all cat owners must learn to deal with.

Cats scratch for several reasons. First, scratching keeps their claws in shape. You schedule a weekly manicure; your cat schedules a scratching session with the sofa. Not only does scratching sharpen the claws and remove the old outer husk of the nail, it just feels good. Think how great it feels when the manicurist massages your hands and arms. Your cat probably gets a similar pleasurable feeling from scratching.

Scratching also serves as a territorial marker. Cats may scratch in preferred sleeping spots or any other place where they spend a lot of time. Doorways and windowsills often get scratched, especially when an indoor cat spots an intruder outdoors. He scratches in a vain attempt to let the other cat know that this is his territory. Scent is another aspect of territorial scratching. The sebaceous glands in a cat's paws leave an odor at the scratched area—another way the cat can stake his claim.

To make sure your cat scratches only in approved areas, think on his level. Cats like to scratch sturdy, vertical objects such as trees. That's why they often choose a chair or sofa as a substitute. Cats like to stretch tall when they claw. Provide your cat with a scratching post that is at least three feet high. This allows the cat to stretch out to his full length, tail included. Cats like to scratch things that are rough. Choose or make a post that is covered in material such as sisal or burlap. Avoid carpet because the cat won't be able to tell the difference between the carpet on the floor and the carpet on the post. Or attach the carpet to the post so that only the rough underside is showing. Some cats like scratching bare wood or logs covered with bark. Provide them with their own small "tree" in the house—a stable log placed so the cat can stand on it and scratch.

To teach your cat to use the post, run your fingernails up and down it. The sound and motion will attract your cat. Sprinkling catnip on and around the post is another good way to heighten a cat's interest, as is giving the cat a treat whenever he scratches in the appropriate place. Always praise your cat when he uses the post, and discourage him with a water squirter when he attempts to use anything else.

Put the scratching post in a convenient area. If you hide it, your cat may not be attracted to it. A corner of the living room or bedroom is a good spot. And beware of moving the post. Cats may protest if you change what they consider the natural order of things.

19

Why Do Cats Spray?

I nquiring minds want to know. Whose territory is this? How long ago was he here? Is she ready to mate? How old is he? Like a distant early warning system, a cat's urine spray contains pheromones—chemical substances that stimulate behavioral responses—that inform other felines of the cat's age, sex, sexual receptivity, and how long ago he passed by. This allows a passing cat to determine whether a rival is in the area and whether to continue on his way or take another route. You might call it a sort of time-sharing arrangement. When the scent from the first cat fades, it's safe for another cat to pass through.

Scent marking also acts as a sign of ownership or as an invitation. When your cat sidles up to a vertical object such as a tree or light pole—or your new sofa—backs up, positions his quivering tail, and emits a pungent spray of urine, he is sending a clear message to intruders: this is mine! Unlike a dog, a cat who comes across the scent mark of another cat will not spray over it. Instead, he makes his mark in a nearby area. On the other hand, female cats in heat spray to indicate their availability. Their urine contains hormones, the scent of which attracts male cats from miles around.

Indoor cats can be just as territorial as their outdoor brethren. It's not uncommon for indoor cats to mark their territory by spraying, especially if there are too many cats in the home or if a new cat is brought into the household. Cats may also claim owner-

If your cat starts spraying in the house, examine your lifestyle for changes. Cats are creatures of habit, and change can cause them to feel the need to state their presence. You can try to prevent spraying by placing aluminum foil or plastic over the area sprayed so that the urine makes a noise or splashes back on the cat; by neutralizing the odor and then feeding the cat in that area (cats don't like to soil their dining rooms); or simply by keeping the cat away from the area. Zap your cat with a water squirter when you see him begin to move into position.

ship of their people by marking areas that smell like their owners.

Unneutered males start spraying at sexual maturity, usually six to eight months of age. To nip spraying in the bud, neuter male cats before six months of age. A neutered cat can still spray if the urge is strong enough, but the odor of his urine is not as powerful. Female cats who are spayed have no need to spray, but they may still go through the motions.

Why Do Cats Bring Us Gifts?

Most of us have always acknowledged to ourselves that cats are superior beings, but now we must accept that our cats know it too. How else can we explain their need to feed us and help teach us to hunt by bringing us gifts of prey? It must concern them that we are so inept at fending for ourselves.

Cats, both wild and domestic, have innate hunting skills that are developed at an early age by the mother cat. She brings food back to her kittens for them to eat, including live prey so they can practice their killing technique. When our cats bring us gifts of prey, it could well be that they are attempting to help us survive. Even spayed females exhibit this behavior. Maybe they are redirecting their maternal instincts to us, their surrogate kittens.

There is another reason that may explain this behavior. Wild cats instinctively bring their prey back to a safe area to eat—a tree or den, for instance.

NKR

For a domestic cat, it may seem only natural to bring her catch to her food dish. After all, that's where she normally eats.

When your cat lines up live locusts on your pillow at six in the morning, or proudly brings a bird to her food dish, accept the gift gratefully. Praise your cat for being such a good provider, then discreetly dispose of the gift. If you would rather not receive any feline bounty, your only option is to keep the cat indoors.

Why Do Cats Make Biscuits?

The American South is known for its colorful colloquialisms and none more so than "The cat is making biscuits": a description of cats "kneading" with their paws. (The saying is especially descriptive for cats with white paws, which look as if they have been dipped in flour.) The reflexive action of pushing the paws in and out on a soft surface harkens back to a time of pure pleasure for most any cat: safe and warm, snuggled up to his mother, kneading as he suckles her warm milk. A cat who is kneading is the very epitome of contentment.

The kneading behavior develops at birth, when the newborn

kitten pushes forward in an attempt to find his mother's nipple and presses with his paws to stimulate the flow of milk. In most cases, it continues throughout the cat's life, appearing during times of relaxation and contentment. We can suppose that the cat who kneads is regressing to a state like that of early kittenhood.

27

Like all mammals, cats are extremely sensitive and responsive to touch. For them, it is an important means of communication. A pleasing touch, such as petting, can easily stimulate kneading behavior. A female in heat kneads in anticipation of mating. Not surprisingly, the cat's forepaws are unusually sensitive (which could explain why so many cats dislike having their paws handled or rubbed).

For humans, few things are as pleasurable as the massage given by a cat's soft paws. Now, if only we could teach cats to keep those claws retracted and to work on sore shoulders and backs.

Why Do Cats Go Wild over Catnip?

Dignity, thy name is cat. No animal has a greater sense of its worth than the regal feline. From the greatest lion down to the tiniest kitten, cats display a degree of self-assurance and pride unparalleled in the animal kingdom.

But one of the few times we see our cats completely lose their dignity is when they are in the throes of a catnip high. They roll and yowl, rub and roll, roll and yowl some more. What is it about this herb that makes it so enticing to cats, so much so that they throw their much-vaunted dignity to the winds? It's the scent.

Catnip, also known as catmint, is a strong-scented herb belonging to the mint family. The effect it has on cats has led some to describe it as a feline aphrodisiac, but strictly speaking, this isn't true. The stimulating effect of this herb is caused by nepetalactone, a hallucinogenic compound that mimics the scent of a cat's sex pheromones. The behavior a cat exhibits while under the influence of catnip is certainly reminiscent of its sexual behavior, but neutered cats display the same behaviors when they're under the

If you would like to grow catnip for your pet, buy some seeds. Fill several four-inch pots with potting soil. Plant 10 to 15 seeds in each pot, and water the soil. Place the pots in a warm, dark area for a few days until the seeds begin to sprout. Then move them to a sunny spot and let the plants grow until there's enough for your cat to start nibbling.

influence. The catnip reaction usually lasts 5 to 15 minutes, with fresh catnip having the strongest effect.

Although we talk about a catnip high, the herb is harmless and nonaddictive to domestic cats, although some wild cats have been known to become addicted to it. In fact, not all cats react to its alluring scent. About one-third of the cat population is immune to catnip's pleasures, as are most kittens.

Why Do Cats Suck Wool?

L ike a baby sucking on a pacifier, your cat may suck on blankets, afghans, or clothing, especially those made of wool. Common in Siamese and Burmese cats (although it is seen in other breeds and mixes), this abnormal nursing behavior is thought to have a number of causes, from a lack of fiber in the diet to stress. One theory suggests that it occurs in kittens weaned too early; thus, they never naturally lost the urge to suckle. Perhaps the scent of lanolin in the wool resembles that of the mother cat's nipple. In the case of Siamese and Burmese cats, wool-sucking may be an inherited behavior.

How can you wean your cat from this annoying, destructive, and potentially dangerous behavior? That depends on why the cat is sucking. Start by offering foods that are high in fiber such as dry cat food, wheat grass, or oats.

If fiber doesn't help, try substituting a toy each time you find your cat sucking on something inappropriate. Praise her when she sucks on the toy instead.

Sometimes, stress is the culprit. You may notice that wool-sucking occurs at certain times. Try to break the pattern by playing with or grooming your cat to replace the sucking behavior.

If all else fails, try prevention. Spray your cat's favorite items with something distasteful such as Bitter Apple. Put woolen items out of reach. (A wool-sucking cat is one way to ensure that clothes stay picked up.)

A cat who merely sucks gently on items made of wool should probably be left alone. Although it's annoying to find small wet spots on your favorite sweater, mildly obsessive sucking isn't really something that should cause serious concern. After all, many cats are neurotic to some degree, and punishing the cat could make the situation worse. The real problem begins when sucking gets destructive. Your cat may wear holes in wool items or even swallow pieces of wool.

A buildup of wool in the stomach can cause serious intestinal obstruction, requiring surgery.

Why Do Cats Roll on Their Backs?

Flop. That's the greeting many cat owners receive when they return home. Snowball runs to the top of the stairs, meows a hello, then falls over in a heap, as if all her bones had suddenly melted. She rolls on her back and extends her paws in welcome.

Surely this is one of the greatest of all cat gifts. When you think about it, a cat who rolls over in greeting is indicating complete trust and faith in the person or animal to whom she is rolling. When a predator such as the cat exposes her belly, she is saying, "I am completely comfortable and contented around you. I know that you would never hurt me." (Not that this means you can always get away with actually rubbing her belly. Often, that requires an even higher level of trust and comfort.)

Cats roll over for a number of other reasons. Sometimes it means they want to play. For a cat-style wrestling match, put a couple of thick athletic socks over your arm and rub your cat's belly. She can rabbit-kick to her heart's content without leaving your arm a bloody mess. (Cats are smart. They learn quickly that this is allowed only when the socks

are in place.) Or pull out the kitty fishing pole and dangle it above her. Watch her roll as she tries to grab the end of the line. When this occurs, your cat may be displaying a form of defensive behavior, albeit in play. A quick roll allows a cat to grasp and claw her adversary.

Rolling is also a form of foreplay. During courtship, the female rolls suggestively, enticing the male with her sinuous movements. You may see the same behavior in a cat high on catnip.

So the next time your cat flops over when you come home, you'll know that you've received the greatest compliment a cat can give: her trust.

Why Do Cats Rub Against Our Legs?

They twine sinuously around our legs, rubbing insistently with their heads. Is this action a demand for food or a friendly greeting? Most of us tend to assume the former, knowing how meaningful meals are to our cats, but what we are actually experiencing is a combination feline greeting and claim of ownership.

Cats have scent glands distributed over their bodies: the perioral glands on the lips and chin, the temporal glands on each side of the forehead, and the caudal glands along the tail. Although the scent emitted by these glands (unlike the scent of cat urine) is undetectable by humans, it serves an important role

in feline and
feline/human social
rituals. One cat
approaching another
raises his tail in greeting.
If the second cat also raises
his tail, the two will then
rub against each other.
In the same man-
ner, cats greet their
people, butting
heads with them or
rubbing up against
their hands or
legs. Not only
is this a friendly

NKR

gesture, it also allows the cat to indicate to all and sundry felines that this person is his. In fact, cats who mark excessively in this way may be nervous or unsure of themselves. So the next time your cat gives you a nice head butt or swirls his tail around your legs, thank him for the compliment, and reassure him that you will always be his devoted love slave.

Why Do Cats Use a Litter Box?

The great thing about getting a cat is that she arrives fully assembled, with no training necessary—except on the part of the owner. Unlike a puppy, who must be painstakingly house trained, a kitten is already programmed by Mom cat to use a litter box. All you have to do is show her where to go.

How did cats come to acquire this neat habit? It's an inborn matter of self-preservation. In the wild, cats bury their feces to hide their presence from predators or territorial rivals. Our domestic house cats continue the habit, which is one of the things that make them such clean companions. The urge to hide

her presence is so strong that even if a cat eliminates outside her box, she will still go through the motions of digging and covering.

Although the litter box habit is deeply ingrained, there are several instances in which a cat may stop using her box. This can lead to a messy situation, but by doing a little detective work, you can soon set your cat back on the proper path.

The first thing to consider is whether your cat is ill. Take Fluffy to the veterinarian for a complete checkup to rule out any physical problems. If Fluffy gets a clean bill of health, make like Sherlock Holmes and consider such elementary factors as cleanliness, type of litter, or household changes. With its sensitive nose, any cat would be turned off by a box that isn't scooped frequently. Cleaning the box of its contents on a daily basis may solve the problem.

Some cats are picky about the type of litter used. Scent and texture are very important to them. If you're using a scented litter, try unscented. If you're using granular litter, consider replacing it with soft, sandlike clumping litter. Such a simple change can make all the difference to our fastidious felines.

If all else fails, try to think of any recent changes that may have stressed your cat. Cats are creatures of habit. A new baby, a new dog or cat, or even a change in household routine can send sensitive cats around the bend. Moving the litter box can be especially problematic. If possible, make changes gradually so your cat will have time to adjust, and give her extra attention to combat her insecurity.

43

Why Do Cats Chatter?

If cats had a theme song for their hunting expeditions, it would no doubt be that anthem of the '70s "Anticipation." That's exactly what's going through a cat's mind when she sees a potential meal flying outside the window. Imagine the feline frustration: "I know I could get that bird, I just know it, and here I am stuck behind this window." It's enough to make a cat gnash her teeth, and that's what she does.

When a cat spots prey, her excitement is told in a swishing tail and chattering teeth. That chatter isn't merely frustration, however. The manner in which the cat is chomping is the same killing bite she would use on prey. In effect, she is carrying out the attack despite her inability to reach her target.

Cats make three general types of sounds--murmurs, vowels, and strained high-intensity sounds—and at least 16 distinct vocalizations, if not more. The chatter, which falls into the category of strained high-intensity sounds, may come from the mother cat's training. She uses much the same sound to alert her kittens to potential prey.

So the next time you see your cat chattering in the window, look out there with her. With your cat's expertise as a spotter, maybe the two of you can take up bird-watching.

Why Do Cats Spend so much Time Grooming?

To a cat, cleanliness isn't next to godliness, it is godliness. No wonder cats spend one-third or more of their waking hours grooming. The grooming ritual begins at birth when the mother cat cleans her babies. It is a way of establishing a powerful social and emotional bond, not only among cats themselves but also between cats and humans.

Although cats have a reputation as independent, standoffish creatures, they have a clear social structure in which touch plays an important role. If you have ever seen a meeting of cats, usually held at twilight on neutral territory, you may have observed them licking each other. Such social grooming is a way of reducing tension in a group situation: the cat's body relaxes, and his heart rate slows.

In addition to its obvious purpose—hygiene—and its social aspect, grooming helps cats cope with conflict. Have you ever seen your cat fall off the bed or caught him doing something forbidden? Usually, the cat's first response is to give himself a few nonchalant swipes with his tongue, acting as if he meant to fall off the bed all along. This type of grooming ritual is called a displacement behavior, and it helps the animal cope with confrontation, conflict, or embarrassment. The act of grooming indicates that all is well.

Some cats groom excessively. Sometimes, these cats are bored, perhaps because they receive little human or feline interaction. These cats suck obsessively at their fur, some even going so far as to mutilate themselves. On the other hand, a sick cat may groom less frequently or stop grooming altogether. Take this as a warning sign and get the cat to a veterinarian.

Last but not least, grooming benefits cats physically. Whether with the cat's rough tongue or the brush of an adoring owner, grooming removes loose hair and parasites such as fleas; stimulates the skin and encourages the growth of new fur; and helps the cat regulate its body temperature through the cooling action of saliva.

To deepen the bond with your cat, set aside a specific time each week for grooming (each day for longhaired cats). Your cat will love the attention, and as a bonus he'll throw up fewer hair balls.

Why Do Cats Play with Their Prey?

A cartoon shows several kittens playing with a mouse when their mother comes along. "Stop playing with your food!" she scolds. Of course, this would only happen in make-believe, not in real life. In reality, kittens learn to kill and eat prey by practicing on live victims provided by their mother. Their habit of seemingly playing with their prey before administering the kill is related to the high level of arousal brought about by the thrill of the hunt. Because cats are attracted by motion, prey that tries to escape may motivate a cat to continue stalking and pouncing until it tires of the game or becomes stimulated enough to deliver the killing bite. When the prey is finally dead, the cat may be so excited that it continues playing with its food.

But not all cats carry through the hunting behavior to its logical conclusion. Hunting and killing are learned abilities. A kitten who doesn't learn these skills from his mother will have no idea how to kill a mouse or bird. Instead, attracted by the sound and movement, he

plays with the animal as he would with a toy. Cats who do learn hunting skills may need the stimulation of stalking and pouncing to trigger the killing instinct. Prey that is inactive may not elicit the fatal bite.

Even if your pet is not a Mom-trained mouser, when you see your kitten or cat pouncing on a ball or chasing his tail, you are seeing prey chasing and catching behaviors in action.

Why Do Cats Hate Getting Wet?

Few things are as amusing as a wet cat. She wears an expression of great disgust as she shakes the wetness from her fur. Then she settles down for a nice long tongue bath to get her coat back in the proper condition, all the while sending indignant glares at the one who dared to bring her to such a pass.

Cats don't have the same protection from water that dogs have. Wet cats take longer to dry because they lack the oily coat and guard hairs that prevent dogs from getting soaked to the skin. But does this mean that all cats hate water? Not at all. Many cats enjoy water and are known to fish and swim for enjoyment.

Throughout literature, many tales are told of cats who like to fish. (Indeed, the cat has its own built-in fishing pole—its tail.) Egyptian hieroglyphics depict cats hunting in marshes with their owners. Cats have been seen hooking trout and other fish out of streams with their paws. Cats have even been observed teaching other cats to fish. So now we know. Cats don't necessarily mind getting wet, but it has to be on their own terms and for their own benefit. Needless to say, a

53

If your cat needs a bath, gather your cat shampoo, towels, and cotton balls, and prepare the water first. The water should be warm, not hot. Put a rubber mat in the bottom of the sink or tub to prevent slipping. Now get the cat. Put cotton balls in the cat's ears to prevent water from running inside them, and place the cat in the water, holding her gently yet firmly. Wet her from the head down, being careful to keep water out of her eyes. Do not dunk the cat in water. Shampoo the cat (never use shampoo made for people or dogs). Next, rinse the cat thoroughly and towel dry her until she is damp. Keep the cat in a warm, draft-free area until she is completely dry.

bath does not fall into either of those categories for the average cat. After all, bathing is what a cat does best—with her own tongue, not with water and shampoo.

Why Do Cats Swish Their Tails?

In addition to their sophisticated vocal skills, cats speak to us in another way: with their tails. To the person fluent in felinese, the movement of a cat's tail can speak volumes, expressing such emotions as happiness, welcome, or anger.

Can you interpret your cat's tail talk? It's a pretty easy language to learn. You can judge your cat's emotional state by the speed and position of his tail. A happy or relaxed cat waves his tail slowly. All's right with this cat's world. A tail held high serves as a greeting. Kittens approach their mothers with tails up, an approach that is perhaps reminiscent of when Mom licked the anogenital area to stimulate elimination. They carry over this body language when greeting humans or other animals.

The tail is even more expressive when the cat is angry, aggressive, or on the defense. A fast-moving tail—swish, swish, swish—denotes annoyance verging on anger. This cat is not happy. It's a good idea to put him down if you're holding him. An aggressive cat crouches with his tail held low. Don't be surprised to see

him swat at or spring on his adversary. The cat under fire uses his tail to fool his enemy. By arching the tail and fluffing his fur, the cat makes himself look bigger and scarier. Sometimes, this posture is enough to make a dog turn tail and run.

Just about every feline mood can be told by the tail. Why is the tail such a versatile means of communication? The answer lies in its skeletal construction. The feline tail has as many as 28 vertebrae, making it mobile indeed. The next time you pull your cat's tail, don't be surprised when he uses it to express his opinion of your ill-mannered behavior.

Why Do Cats Eat Plants?

P lant life is the last thing we would expect a carnivore to eat, yet eating greenery is one of the most common behaviors of cats. They nibble delicately on plants and flowers, partaking of leaves and petals as if they were enjoying the most delicious of salads. Then they throw up on the special carpet that great-aunt Muriel brought back from the Orient.

Many of us become greatly concerned when our cats eat plants. Not only must we deal with green stains on the carpet, we also worry about our cats eating poisonous plants. Among the most common poisonous house and garden plants are dieffenbachia, English ivy, oleander, and philodendron.

Eating plant parts may fulfill an instinctive need for greenery in the diet. Wild cats eat every part of their prey, including the grassy contents of their stomachs. Many theories have been proposed to explain this habit. It could be that grass provides fiber or certain vitamins and minerals not found in meat. Another possibility is

To meet your cat's need for greenery, grow him a box of oats or wheat grass of his very own. This may prevent him from chewing on houseplants—which isn't very good for the plants—and it is a healthy alternative to eating grass outdoors, which may be treated with pesticides or infested with parasite eggs. Follow the directions given on page 31 for growing catnip.

that grass helps the cat rid his system of hair swallowed during grooming. Whatever the reason, with the exception of harmful plants, eating greenery is a pretty harmless activity. As far as we can tell, cats do it just because they like it.

Why Do Cats Like Crinkly Sounds?

Cats love crinkly sounds. Try crumpling a plastic or paper bag and watch your cat's ears snap to attention. Like her tail, the cat's ears are expressive, twitching and turning to catch each unusual sound. The same thing happens when a cat hears a squeaky toy or any high-pitched sound. Part of the pleasure a cat gets from crawling into a paper bag comes from the sound it makes.

Is there a reason these types of noises elicit greater interest than others? Of course! Our mighty feline hunters rely almost as heavily on their ears as on their eyes. Crinkly or squeaky sounds are similar to the high-frequency noises made by small animals such as mice, birds, and crickets; thus, they immediately draw a cat's attention and often elicit the prey response of pouncing and stalking.

A cat's ears are always on alert. Even when she's sleeping, you may notice a slight twitching of the ears in response to a sound that might indicate danger. When it comes to hearing, cats have it in the bag.